Chokey

Chokey

Rosy Carrick

Burning Eye

Burning Eye Books
Never Knowingly
Mainstream

This edition published by Burning Eye Books 2018

www.burningeye.co.uk

@burningeyebooks

Burning Eye Books
15 West Hill, Portishead, BS20 6LG

ISBN 978-1-911570-39-4

Printed & bound by ImprintDigital.com, UK

For my dear friend
James Burt

'And you, you will come too, young brother; for the days pass, and never return, and the South still waits for you. Take the Adventure, heed the call, now ere the irrevocable moment passes! 'Tis but a banging of the door behind you, a blithesome step forward, and you are out of the old life and into the new! Then some day, some day long hence, jog home here if you will, when the cup has been drained and the play has been played, and sit down by your quiet river with a store of goodly memories for company. You can easily overtake me on the road, for you are young, and I am ageing and go softly. I will linger, and look back; and at last I will surely see you coming, eager and light-hearted, with all the South in your face!'

Kenneth Grahame, *The Wind in the Willows*

CONTENTS

PIG/OWNER

One of us is the pig and one of us is the owner.
You can be the owner first
but you need to find at least five ways to slaughter me
or else it isn't fair.

That's not how it goes anymore.
Now you can be a cat
or a chicken
or anything.
It's better because you get to choose how you want to die.
Cats like to be stroked,
so you could lure me onto your lap,
cut off my tail with a pair of scissors,
slice off all my fur
and have me put down.

You can't really do that with a chicken.
But chickens like the sound of seed in a bucket
and will follow it into the dark shed where you could
laser off my beak and toes,
pull my feathers out one at a time
and flay my whole skin off
with some twigs
wrapped round with barbed wire
and probably also acid.

Wear gloves.

REGARDING THE KEY:

I believe that it has to be wrong.
Every day I have forced it,
at every degree, and
even on Friday
scraped all the skin off my right thumb's knuckle
on your front door –
it will never go in.
Of course
I walk the outside of your porch
each morning and evening
and push fresh meat through the mailbox for Tom,
though I panic a little at this –
at maggots and mould
if he isn't a quick enough eater.

To save your documents rotting, I lie to the postman:
I confiscate anything bearing your name
and tell him I see you for coffee each morning,
though this is by no means ideal –
he's a trickster for timing –
some days I clean miss him by seconds
and others am sucked into pacing your path for an hour or more
until he arrives.
The man himself is a very curious bird.
I tell you that when he is staring,
and often he is,
with his
straightened teeth,
his narrow veins and lazy sleeves,
I feel most strange at your door –
indeed it is tricky
to push soft meat through a letterbox cleanly
and act all the while as though it were nothing but paper.

On such days that he lingers
I'm forced to confess it out loud:
I'm chasing an empty house!
I say that perhaps you forgot me,
you're often a rather cruel, ineffective friend –
and with my back to him then I am canny:
I cram any letters I'm holding
into the hole I cut
into my coat lining
and with my mouth in the shape of a smile
walk by him,
adrenaline baiting my guts out of torpor,
though like a magician I torture the thought
that something
is waiting to fall.

PAIN SPECIFIC

A corporeal mincing of, in this machine.
Each roughened crank turned
by milky owls,
their heads at right angles and eyeless.
A sure slow thing – boiled alive from frozen,
the body flung over in
    tar
but lighter,
    more viscous than –
less terrific smelling, and closer to petrol
for potential.
An *actual* machine –
nothing metaphorical about it –
to get strapped into.
Black lead lid,
the sense of rust where there is none.
Howling out of it,
all organs in gangbang implode to be exploding;
frequent fear of limb loss where dead skin leads the way;
fluoroantimonic acid on hand to sculpt the stubborner gristle
    baby smooth –
give
    this
       round of applause
               to the living torso!
Striking a match with its teeth, scorching
its lips off,
soothing everything better on – what –
the wet of its tongue?
As sodium
punches water,
from the tears: tight gut, protruding bones and eye bags.
Compulsion for photographic proof of –
from flattering angles in spite of –
can't even
wank over the thought of what we –
your –

wretched retraction forces itself
                              a virus
into memory:
hot skin, line of the jaw,
what the hell – I held your face, looked into your eyes,
do people do that in real life?
Victorian electrocution
device.
Hot skillet
        of plastic –
                      sharded,
applied to the solar plexus.
To tighten the jaw,
to fail to maintain physical integrity, being:
violin strings between scissors,
smell of rubber,
the new Scorsese,
cheese wire
(what it might *and might not* cut through),
screw driver:
the brutalist assault to slash this map
north to south,
north-east to south-west
and south-east to north-west.
Re-move
some other land.

VANISHING ACT

The hunger is the proof I can do it.
I scrabble the bony bits all of the time,
evicting the meat of my body.
I press my ankles and knees together
and stand
with a lit lamp behind me
fully naked in front of the mirror,
then use my hands to cup up and squeeze back tight
the top of each anxious thigh.
The possibility of all this extra light
from between my legs
makes excitement beat in my gut
and steadies my aim.
I photo my torso from every angle
in each degree of shadow,
edifying ribs
and stroking clean the breastbone.
All of a sudden I've been at it close to a day,
every night is the same,
though it's only the best when it's clear that I'm shrinking in
earnest
and then I am lost.
The lameness of fat – I get it
around my hips,
heavy as horse collar,
it needles the truth:
I'm a greedy girl.
Unphysical.
I eat beyond the point of sustenance.
Sometimes I think my aim is to be muscular,
easily run ten miles or climb a rope like children do,
but knowing the magic of growing smaller
remains the unspeakable truth.
Ideally
I would scrape around,
an optical illusion or a skeleton in skin

with just
I guess
sufficient muscle left to reach a destination.

MAYAKOVSKY

After waiting an hour full of anxious belly for my photo
in this darkroom
I remember
the man I am waiting for is dead
and is not a photographer.

And then he arrives,
massive in the doorway,
and roars nonstop about love is life and the night
cigarette is the saddest
and where his puppy Schenik's run away to.

I mime answers,
terrified,
tipping reclined
on his last Rodchenko chair
and it becomes very soon clear he's forgotten
he sits a death mask yellow
in his antique, love
letter-lined Moscow museum
and should I be the one to break it?

I take him outside
to show best where the birds shit over my washing,
where he is incensed at tree surgeons working overhead –
bulleting orders up at the branches:
Listen up!
All you chainsaw-holding hands
now hack away at your opposite hands
and then at each other's –
and now –
each to be sewn back on in a mixed-up order
so that all of you might give in
to a stranger's stroke tonight!

They reply by a blizzard of shavings,
wood-chips whipping our eyes,
relentless,
swelling our mouths;
he empties his tongue in a spit,
and for a second
the woodchips hover
to form the shape of an elderly Russian,
but he doesn't see it,
demanding we chew up a pack of tobacco,
slapping his thighs
and firing wisecracks back at each invisibly raucous passer-by;
the only retort I can muster,
to quietly sidle back into the darkroom;
a loneliness in love,
I watch my face developing in paper.

EQUIPOTENTIAL BONDING

You remember our infantile slicing through
and thrusting up of grass with spades,
and that
ambivalent smack of sublime
at our loot of bewildered worms
sucking into themselves in chill –
and here, one a little pulped in our haste –
and here,
one cut clean up?
Your skull,
in all its severable sections,
has me snapping the bones of my thumbs
in the glee of a power surge
similar.

The rigid root of the neck
and that base section of scalp
to the left –
my throat rams tight,
I sweat at the very remembrance –
matte and bare your metal,
cold and dimple-free your form,
my fingers
flex
and cram
and rip through their nails
at your too-stiff seams –
your flick switch, your
release catch
keeping hidden.
I adore the torture of losing its location – but
there.

Dinted and stainless steel,
you defeat me:
I peel back your lid
and crackling wires I tug
and wrap into my hands,
electricity-burnt
and dancing with shock-nipped ecstasy,
scooping out like fruit this bronchiole mass.
And how the lights in your sockets flicker and spasm,
your split consumer units bursting their fuses –
movement jagged –
you jerk you –
crack out at my cheekbone with an elbow inadvertent:
your malfunction.

Pocked and stupid now
you flay out fits,
you crumple beneath me;
hammered concave each knobbling
spinal segment
and smashed
from protrusion to hollow the hips,
you sing
with pale scratching lines
like the trails of snails
where I sought
and failed
to carve you apart with a hacksaw.

TIME MACHINE

I push always forwards
with my body and my work
and I am happy this way –
I've never been inclined to kick through the rizla
and see what my parallel worlds might look like.
There is nothing
I wish I had never done, or
had just done differently;
I trust in myself,

but like anyone alive
I have my regrets:
I am sorry for the things that were done to me
that can never be undone;
I am sorry that they trail me,
that they tie me to dates that can't be forgotten;
I am sorry that they wait till I'm sleeping my deepest
to make me spring out of my bed in a panic
and roil my nerves in adrenaline.

It's no lie
to say that good can come from bad
if you work at it forcefully.
I remind myself often
how now
I am powerful,
now I am safe,
but you know sometimes when you sit at your desk,
surrounded by your skills,
and despite it all
feeling
extremely alone –
translating
a poem for a play you know
you're too afraid to act in
and regressing so stupidly teenage,
the forearm begging for a sliver of broken glass

so it can cry the way it needs to,
bitter second to the rubber band
that flocks up your skin like wallpaper,
that puts you
nose to nose
with your terrible truth –

and you are tired
of the injustice
of the energy
that you need to produce
just to be pushing always forwards,
to keep you from circling back there.

A BLITHESOME STEP FORWARD

Dearest ankle,
stuck like a prick between a shoe and a trouser
in a blue ribbed Marks & Spencer sock,
if it were not that I am only eyes incapable of being taken off
you
and you are tibia fibula talus robotics,
if I were a human
and you were too,
I would lovingly spit
and destroy you.

Aren't you sick
of being trapped in that blue sock
like a baby?
Don't you buckle instead to be naked
and scathingly licked by a tongue
with no recourse to thinking
to make it stop?

Is that clonic seizure flex on purpose?
The veins might try
to eke out their metre
but that sock,
frankly,
is skin-tight,
and you protrude so livid and
bonily pulsar.

How about this?

I've got a bunched-up pair of keys at the ready and unless
you convince me with solidly desperate humiliating passion
– bannable under the new porn laws – that your mortice is so
stable that a deity could be aborted in it and no one would
kick up a fuss, I will stab them into you and hack you apart –
below from the deeply embarrassing neediness of your foot;
above from the ugly black dog of your calf – and I will

henceforth cuddle the residual ligamentous stump of you into
the heart-hand side of my bra.

Forgive the height
of my insensitive impatience.
I know
an ankle
has no mouth to answer with
and inescapably
in any case
of course I am plagued
(who could not be?)
by terror –
that to force such a change on an ankle like that,
to render it lumpen
with no foot to,
with muscular purpose,
make me observe how
for exercise purely
it marches away so briskly,
might
(might it not?),
though turmoil persuades me violently otherwise,
make it look rather suddenly useless,
drained of its animal blood.

I don't buy that, obviously.
After all, if worms, cut into pieces,
just get on with it with whatever's left
and delight, even, who knows,
in the breeze afforded their severed ends,
then—

Plus, there is something to be said for refusing to relinquish
the torment of unprofitability.
I am more,
after all,

than arousingly
a pair of peeled eyes and, with that,
daily I mourn in the riveted flesh for the items I know to be true:
that I
myself
will never
tenderly hammer
the ankle dressed in blue
into my cheekbed
or grab it for fun in public
and Chinese burn it over my knee.

By the laws,
in short,
which govern this ankle,
which this ankle,
motherfucking powertripper,
gagging to be king of everything,
itself stipulates,
I am caused
insomniac suffering.
The screaming skin between the sock and the trouser's hem,
minutely exposed
when the ankle is shifting position, is a thing
I will die
having never discovered the taste of
and, worse yet,
there is no permissible context for my thumb
without warning
to slip inside the sock's elastic
and rub round the imprint left by it.

If I were to rearrange my pelvis,
let's say,
to friction
my brown boot against the shoe below the
blue-socked ankle I'm sick without

when one of us moves,
as an act of necessary transference,
I would be stuttered by the bluntness of their coarse soles,
and knowing I had
so publicly
burned alive my only card
I would make a show of just how I had said I would
linger
and look back
for the ankle not mine
and be mortified.

WUNDT'S LAW

Look,
it seems clear that nothing will come from this particular attempt,
so I advise you to just stop trying,
right now.
Put on your shoes and take a stroll outside instead.
Imagine how things could be
outside.
You might see a shop
and decide to buy a banana or a book,
a 50p bargain bin book maybe –
ragged-looking but with the kind of title you can't not go for:
You Too Will Die Last Week, or *Magic, and How to Undrink It*.
If the day is sunny, and it is,
the park is close.
Right now
you could be in that park,
biting into a soft banana
and reading the opening pages of a book so like a god
in its clear understanding of all your sturdiest fears
that you will race back home
only to collect your dental floss and passport,
and will take a train to the airport
without even thinking a single thought the whole of the journey,
just reading and reading,
and sometimes
for a break
looking out of the window,
and then you will be there,
and you will book a ticket on the next available flight –
all basic inoculations and visa requirements allowing –
and you could even now be getting onto that plane
and as it sets off,
as it tips itself backwards
and as your ears steel themselves for the popping
and everything in you twists with terrific excitement
for all of the streets in the world that wait to be walked through,
and all the films you'll see at tiny cinemas with strangers,

and all of the alien alcohols and chocolate bars and beetles,
you will remember
very suddenly
Wundt's law regarding excitement –
you will remember that too much excitement is a wholly
    unpleasurable item:
being attacked on the street,
falling from a building in bare knees
and so on,
and you will know absolutely you are headed for that –
you are in that, even,
and that this is not a good or positive challenge,
it is a terrible *terrible*,
so you will stand and scream,
and make to punch the people around you,
announcing all the while the intention to kill
and to cut off the hair from all unfriendly heads
until the decision is made to reland the plane –
and it will be relanded
and passengers will make you
with their eyes
and their wringing hands
feel very guilty
and you will run,
following your police caution, your confiscated dental floss
and threats of several fines –
run to the train –
from the station to the house –
nakedly ball up –
discover the stench of your armpits –
double lock
every one
of the windows
and doors
and jump inside of a hot and silent bath.

THE DOLLS' HOUSE

Joking aside, I'm dying.
The door keys are kept on top of the shoe rack, there's
a cake in the fridge,
but I made it myself so it might be that nobody wants it,
and there are the neighbour's cats,
who come to the window on Tuesdays
for tuna scraps:
Bubble and Squeak.

To my mother
I want to say sorry.
The day I bought that plum box when we were cleaning the
    house
the day we moved out
and you thought I'd used my own money,
I hadn't.
I'd taken a pound from your purse,
which I had *said* I was going to do but you mustn't have heard,
and you seemed so proud
that I'd bought them for you all on my own,
I couldn't bring myself
to be truthful.
I thought:
when I'm on my deathbed, then I'll confess it,
and I couldn't forget.

BETRAYAL OF THE WORKERS

As you know,
my daily ritual is to make you die in my body
and work with what's left,
and so when this morning
I was puking out my hangover
and telling Ashley
with absolute outrage and anger
how our friend had washed off his marriage
and tried his luck at my unrelenting crotch
for the sake of some remnant of intensity
his cock had conjured up,
it came instinctively to me
to reimagine
and grapple the rapturous certainty
that had it been you and I that night;
if he and I were the ones engaged,
and mine the baby new enough to count its life
in weeks and days;
if you,
rumbling drunkly,
post-poetry,
crammed into Rachel's bed out of necessity,
did not seek to remove my creeping hands
crassly masquerading as the comfort stroke of friendship
across your torso;
if you strained your ribs a smidge against my fingertips,
displayed the slightest hint of lust
about your moving shape,
or kept your breath till silence grew ambiguous,
I too would, without
a second's hesitation,
have expunged the very existence of those
whose photos,
only hours ago,
I'd broken down for strangers on the tube
as I set the trembling thunder of my belly to work
undressing you.

You operate better naked, by night;
by day you get as nervous as you are clothed,
and so I am skilled in manufacturing
sharp transitions
from apodyopsis to strip search strategy –
gagging to ogle you properly
today like tomorrow like yesterday.

The shyness of your nape
I would isolate,
force to take cover in my mouth
as a traveller,
distorted by walking,
rests the nights in caves for safety.
I would mother your discomfort by methods
untenable by sunlight,
bless and consecrate the knuckles of your spine beneath my
    silent breath
and make an inchoate crime of your skin
whose further corruption mine would insist on,
sealing into every pore my sorry prayer of gratitude
and tempering our sentence
by changing the laws of morality to suit us.
I would play out to your gaping hands
with my breasts
the secrets of their destiny,
and all of the leftover body bits that never get to act sexy
I would party at:
the heels of the feet,
the outer edges of ears,
kneecaps bulging with cartilage, translucent;
make them too feel
porn-like as the frames of the Stations of the Cross must do.

But in doing so,
in deserting my truth and my family,
I would debase myself,
I would make myself as unworthy as you
have always been of my worship,
therefore
I will step down,
trying not to look long at you,
as if you were the sun,
yet I will see you,
like the sun,
even without looking,
and the torture will not bear speaking out loud,
will not bear insisting
into the shadows all shaking their withering heads
the petulant gospel
that you and I
transcend the name betrayal,
and so for the sake of all my holy frothing riot,
homeless and desperate,
I beg you:
please climb back inside me
and die in my body again.

FERROEQUINOLOGY

*'Trainspotting may be an activity of limited, and indeed
questionable, appeal, but it is not a criminal offence and it
is not a terrorist threat.'*

Norman Baker, 2009

The uniform
commonly worn by the British trainspotter
is not compulsory,
though its basic components *are* nevertheless
formally recommended in all preliminary notes to
TLX – an excellent resource
for any earnest ferroequinologist,
the current edition of which
features recently unearthed early photos by my father,
Jeremy Foster.
He's been dead for years, *of course*,
but here is the thing:
last Monday I caught the train from Boston to Lincoln,
it was winter – there was snow on the ground –
and this man on the platform blowing out his cheeks
looked right through me
and there was my answer.

At first I thought I was dreaming –
he had both logbook *and* a tape recorder,
mic attached on a headset,
three spare pens in left breast pocket,
waterproof trench,
and even anyweather trousers
(ankle-length, they button up
or else just zip off altogether at the thigh).
Timetables fanned from a clam-tight armpit
and behind his glasses railroadiana nostalgia flashed
like it was now and he was juggling yesterday,
but before I got the chance to un-agog my tongue,
to let him know

I knew
we fit like puppy and dog,
he ran across to the very far side
(the train from Newark,
hours delayed,
was being announced on platform 2
and he was eager to see it arrive).

I threw away my Twix and followed him over.
Stepping inside of his footprints,
I leant forward,
rested my ear on his shoulder,
sniffed his neck
and stroked the Woolworth's data notepad tucked into his thick
    belt.
It did not go well.
I guess it's okay to feel defensive – spinning around,
he spat this rant against my face, like:
Fuck you, bitch!
This –
all you think –
I'm not a freak, you know!
I just
love trains! Just
live for this machinery, not
cracked in the head – not
trackbasher bent – and yes, I
do do other things as well –
I go to parties – I eat pizza! Like to dance
and drink
and screw!

To take my mind off his teeth
I thought of that Pulp song too
and began to imagine our wedding day –
how we would talk of this first meeting during the speeches,
recreate its brilliant drama word for word –

not even edit it clean for the children or elderly relatives.
Then, kneeling down at his feet in the snow,
my tongue as hot as Shakira,
I asked him:
Please will you make me a chokey
like the one Miss Trunchbull has
in that Roald Dahl book called *Matilda*?
Full of nails
and broken glass
and me inside
all cut to bloody
stranded naked –
standing straight for hours in the dark?

The silence made my clothes fall off,
a tortoise in my chest,
and he said finally:
But what about my almost-crippling fondness for machinery?
Surely you don't think
a vintage train aficionado
has the time
to build this chokey just for you?
Thinking fast like a special agent,
I said:
Don't you know my face? You know
my father's Jeremy Foster?
That makes you my legal guardian
according to the railway etiquette of '62,
and he,
beginning to cry, said:
Then I guess I'll have to try to.

Then the Newark train arrived
and he recorded its model and number next to the time,
and I got back to my feet
and brushed the snow away from my bruised knees
and touched his cheek
as his face jerked
and his hot sperm
shot through those twitching pants that later my hands
ecstatic
would start to remove.

THE INTRUDER

This uninvited woodlouse picking through my inner ear
must have torn its door in the drum while I was sleeping,
stretched it exoskeleton-wide
and crawled inside.

I think it rolled its shell in a slug's trail first
because its perforation left no ache or swelling,
just the certainty
of close and tiny company
for when that heavy flesh arrives to blindly wrap around.

Those old
bad feelings
seem unthinkable now –
it's truly all of a magical spell –
we love to listen to Chopin and Rachmaninoff,
and I
shrug off my skull,
make my torso screech intractable as billy-o
to roll it
high and circular,
then jerk a ragged beat,
as my woodlouse,
spinning ecstatic in its hot cave,
makes, from close
muffled shudder-reposition
to freefall,
my reeling agent.

And when I sense a pining for its former world,
I press my ear to the night-time ground
and drown my bony labyrinth in trembling occupation.
Blithely steeped in this reverberating offering,
it dreams alive my
lost incorporation lullaby.

(TO KEEP INVESTMENT INTENTIONS SECRET)

Introducing
a volatile skin, tipped
under wraps as capital un/confirmed
with emphasis *clear* that it is systematically
unclear
when to snap up a stake amidst such
forwarded performance options as:
withdrawn proposals
and
avoidance of detailed strategy
about working alone or in partnership.
This latter,
the fundamental branches of which
have amassed more than tangible assets:
vast swathes of complex derivatives
rebranded as such tourist destinations as:
Excessive Pessimism,
Potential Disposal
andSLASHor
Economic Worry
in spite of high interest – if
high risk – if
significantly, *almost irredeemably* flawed
macro-aggressive attraction.

HEART

Look,
we all know you were born with a hole in your heart
and that when the doctor sewed it closed
she lost a hair from her head across the top of your aorta
and so now you dream of her childhood every night,
but that's no excuse for cutting away from your family
and quitting your job –
you eat like an animal!
All this meat every morning for breakfast –
you can't grow a second heart,
you know,
by twicing the scope of your skin –
there's now a graveyard of pigs' ears
in pet shops
whose body bits got hacked off on your account,
and it wasn't like this ten years ago.

When you bring up the hair over dinner,
this magical, endlessly static, non-disintegrating hair,
and your plans
to have it CAT scanned
and removed
so you can stop feeling guilty for never going to visit
her brother's ashes,
I can see the faces of couples at neighbouring tables,
rolling their eyes uncomfortably into their soup
as you spit grease across the tablecloth in your passion,
their scorn aimed always at me
for humouring this nonsense,
as though
even to be in your company
and not be trying to shut you up
is a form of neglect in the face of your clear psychosis.

When the months pile up wrongly
and I fall back on the tracks of that terrific low
where everything's more like the smear of crushed slug

on escalator
(grey)
than a bucket
full of endless hot chocolate and TV,
you lose sight of me in the face of her
difficult days at school
and how her father never called her back
when he said that he would do
and I buy into it:
playing along in the part of her best friend,
I talk to you sleeping
and you are clearly so beside yourself
to speak to me then –
in clumsy, muttered REM conversations you squeeze
my hand
like a treadling cat
and when you cry
through your lashes,
terrified
of these recurring dreams you get
of being an ageing fat man
with a wife
whose arms are
covered
in snail-trail scars,
I reassure you
that *those people have never existed*,
and stroke tidy your flailing eyebrows
as we thicken the braid of our future plans
for the pictures
on the walls
of the bagel shop
we're going to open together
as soon as we've grown up.

STAMMER

Repay
Rapesco
Reap
Parental
Nape

Pare down
Window pane
Pare back
Hope

Pager
Tape player
Real
Rare
Paper cut

Papal authority quizzed
New pope named
Rampant
Old rope

Rupee down
Rapturous
Rates inflate

Rap Entwhistle's knuckles
Bare

Riots rage in England
Rasping
Outrage

Grope

Grapple
Grapefruit
Green grapes
Capers

Ripe
Radical
Drapery
Capes

Rapacious
Pipe
Report force repeal

Newspaper
Parody
Panicking
Rapid

Release
Agape face
Rupture

Repeat.

HOLDING HANDS

Walking back to the new flat after the Odeon,
our hands meet in my pocket
and at last there is no love in it,
just awkwardness;
it's cumbersome
and all of the sex I used to get from stroking the length of your
     palm has gone
and I wish I'd never
cut the thing off in the first place –
it was tricky to do,
much harder than it looks in the movies
and messier too –
too meaty a fit for the pockets of all of my coats,
except for that old grey duffel we found outside Barnardo's
and *you know* I don't like to wear that if I can help it –
it stinks
and scratches my neck with its collar
and even in this,
I reach in and find it all of a tangle inside;
it gets in the way of everything –
think I've located my lighter,
turns out it's one of your fingers –
you know the drill.

So I take it out,
play catch with it a little,
give it a kiss,
and make the decision to leave it behind in the park
by my new street
but the scar on your right thumb
straight away turns into
a screaming mouth,
and the roughened skin on the heel of your palm starts to grizzle
like a cabasa
and my pocket now feels like a ravenous cave
with bad things spilling out of it.
I can't help it –

I run back,
grab the hand from its seat
and smother the whole thing cheek to cheek across my face.

I make it ruffle my hair again;
I kiss every knuckle
and chew away a few of the longer nails,
and when I do get home
I wrap the fingers together in Sellotaped cling film tightly,
unlikely to ever mistake them again
for something that needs to be found.

THE FILM

On the inlaid ceiling TV screens
of the train back home to Moscow
from St Petersburg
a film began.
It was identical
in colour, scale and focus
to the films I used to watch on Sundays as a child
which used to make in me
at that
inflammable age
insane excitement,
followed quickly by a gripping attrition of bodily sickness
and bettered only
by long explicit lectures
at church
in primary school
of Jesus's crucifixion,
and how
alone in my bedroom,
rigid with fear of discovery,
I fantasised the scenes of my demise;
would split myself in two
and force the guilty half
to lie face down
with pieces of sharpened plastic,
felt-tip pens driven into the stomach,
having not discovered yet the interests of my puppeteering
cunt
within the play.

Films of sailors
and robbers
and strong-willed persons
toplessly flogged unconscious
and keelhauled,
screaming and bleeding into the open stupefaction
of my mouth,

and so, in my seat today,
nostalgically I waited for the whips to come,
but here in Russia,
nothing but guns and running away –
the film itself became to me
a form of torture
of most perverse unsettling sorts,
which finally charged a frantic resort to reading
online
on my mobile,
via the Sapsan WiFi –
like some kind of futuristic version of my pre-teen self
who, desperate for specifics,
would scan the family encyclopaedia:
T for torture –
historical documents
detailing how on the C19th prisoner ship *Success*
the men were brutally, frequently beaten,
        and by what means.

Later,
having availed myself of the compact train facilities
to wank in,
uncomfortably,
and fighting the feeling of being slightly soiled by
or soiling of
this pristine environment,
I got back into my seat
where,
straight away,
the man on my right leaned over
and as if in recognition
of my silenced childhood self,
the isolation of games that could not be described to my friends

and the times my mother told me off for marks she found on
     my body
whilst washing my hair in the bath,
which were,
I could not bring myself to say to her,
no self-endangering symptoms
but a basic glorification of flesh
and its capacity for degradation,
holy shame
and pure immortal ecstasy,
as if in reward for my low-grade
compulsory
sexual innovation
in the face of Russian cinematic adversity,
he handed me a Twix
and said:
I bought this one for you.

PASSPORT

The first day I saw you I knew you were the one,
so when my new passport arrived in the post
I entered your information
into the space for emergency contacts.
As soon as I had saved enough money
you received
on a sheet of eBay-purchased State Department paper
the primary notice:
'Rosy Carrick has had a misfortune
in the Jacuzzi room
of the honeymoon suite
of a five-star hotel in Paris.'
Waiting, I felt so fantastically girlish,
but my money ran low
and my skin became pruned to an unattractive measure
before you could make it.

In the following years
I broke my legs in the Philippines,
had panic attacks in Papua New Guinea
and ate a selection of poisonous plants in Brazil.
I cancelled all of my travel insurance
and Googled a list of dangerous places for tourists to travel
alone.
I rehomed my dog.
Twice I was forced to halt my campaign
for reasons too shameful to talk about.
With one year remaining,
I arranged to have one of my hands taken off
by a street gang in Oslo
in return for maintaining that I was a rival
who simply had got what was coming.
The hand made it onto the internet
but despite my best efforts
the police succeeded in keeping my identity secret.

It's painful,

to be always the one who is waiting.
It triggers my
vulnerabilities,
and restricted mobility
means that I can't just run them away like I used to.
But I look forwards –
I imagine you,
skimming the surface of the earth like a fury,
the emergency contact for everyone living,
the pressure of who to save first
and on which day.
I admire you fervently.
I will keep a hold of my pain now
and wait for my turn.

DISAPPEARING LADY

We start like giants:
I
pushing hard to the rolling meat of her belly,
she
mountain-like,
tight-skinned and violently
impatient.
Soon, as though we are brawling,
she pulls hard at my shoulders and flips me to her side like a
    dinghy capsizing,
our torsos pinched and winded –
my influx of breath a reflex
as her thigh leans
and threatens to snap my pelvis.
We disentangle and I,
flung back,
brace myself for support
and grow terror in the face of her pink and folding form
that she will split like the top of a muffin
and swallow me down entirely,
but she grows smaller.

A trick of the shadows, surely?
The darkness in here
cracks caverns across her hips
but in flicking the lamp on to check
I disrupt her thrusts and prove myself a fool:
she is shrinking for real –
and now angry.
She slaps my face –
she bellows my faults
and this makes her tinier still;
at each forward thump of her pelvis to mine
she gets lighter,
her lips
a towering halo
crowning the muscular trunk of her tongue.

She clamps her hands around mine –
my initial assumption: a gesture of romance,
before she jams up the Vs of my thumb and forefinger lines to
    the nook of her larynx,
my fingers like crocodile teeth behind at her sweaty nape.
I squeeze
until her lips are prickling purple,
until her head bows low,
her arms are dangling limply to my chest;
she has the face of an angel
drowning like this
and even as I watch she grows as small as a baby,
a fervent blur,
she rubs herself slick,
her eyes strain to a globular close
and then
there is nothing of her at all –
and I fall in on myself
in a fit of disbelief,
fingers fumbling the empty air, white
and each tip ablaze with a glorious grievance
like the site of some small tear,
my visceral organs, balloons untethered,
rising in the wake of her weight,
an empty whisper, catching like split stitches,
her sole remains:
I am here.
I am come.

BENEFACTED

Dear Arnold,
it's tough being poor
when you're a single mother
with a taste for rubber,
funding your own PhD
on a poet nobody's heard of
in a language nobody speaks –
but now you have granted the SodaStream
we can make as much champagne as we can manage,
the seeds we need for our undernourished skin
we'll steal from Tesco
and the parmesan for our cut-price tinned ravioli
we will cultivate
between the toes
of our children's fertile feet.
This evening,
in the name of *Terminator*s
1 and *2* and *Genisys*,
we will feast like queens.

Last week it was not so easy.
I was desperate for a cup of tea
but the new red kettle Jake had bought me
to replace the crap one from Maxine
was acting exactly like a terrible lover –
it kept on flicking its switch off
before my water was *close* to boiling
so that on three, maybe four occasions
I had to forcibly hold it down to keep it going.
At times like that I long for tobacco
but I haven't smoked since I broke up with Adam –
for real this time –
I couldn't trust my resolve to be rid of him
and needed to do something concrete
as a sign of my commitment.
Jewellery
I couldn't afford,

and I knew I'd only pretend to like it,
hide it in a cupboard awkwardly
and eventually give it away to someone whose tastes
I don't understand –
perhaps even myself without thinking –
a Secret Santa isn't the same when you work in isolation.
It was just too much,
so the cigarettes bit the dust instead
and now I am fully faithful to my mouth
but gagging to suck on something deadly again
while I have my flashes of genius.

I know you know distractions
like Red Army herrings
rear their heads.
It's hard when you have to somehow get through
all 937 pages
of Trotsky's
The History of the Russian Revolution
if that sweaty,
formerly home-educated twenty-year-old
you taught last year
who wears tights underneath his ripped jeans
in support of the proletariat
will ever want to have sex with you,
when at every third page you alternately
fall asleep
or give in to your compulsion to masturbate
so that every night is insomnia-riddled
in ripe sheets
with fingers puckered
more profoundly than a Walkers Deep Ridged crisp.
But then
you'll always be a bodybuilder first,
and this is my curse as a desperate woman
who works predominantly from home.
It's impossible to be discreet about one's feelings

in the real world
when the very sight of the beloved object
makes you literally gut yourself with recyclables
and the only advice your mother ever gives you is:
Well, Rose,
you know what they say about people in your condition:
Bound Bitch Jerks Meat.

DOG

It's you,
of course,
my own sweet cage,
I privately chant you –
thank mercy for all of my long-extinct diaries,
for this empty page to hide you in,
my love,
you rubble, you
ransack me;
my rib shack in ruins,
I condemn you to these lines only –
force you in
between
dead lists and letters,
the punctured expression of your face,
your juddering mouth,
the straightforward features of your terror,
desire indelible – I
lick the seams,
seal you in with elastic and black tape,
your
intensity painful,
I adore you.
Keep me
please
somewhere hidden too.
When everything else is deleted
keep me folded
tiny,
hardy as linseed
and strip me,
read me,
unravel me,
remembering how,
as you shake off the night,
I am keeping you always
base

and alive,
I will draw you the tenderest kennel
to rest in,
my festering
prison,
my terrible secret,
my friend.

THICKENING WATER

I shake.
My eyes are stinging with tears
and the blood that lies
visibly
under the surface of arse and thighs,
around ribs,
begins the pin-prick trickle
as you split the skin open
with each timed flick of the whip.
Trying to scream,
cleaving
like raw meat hacked off the bone
the soaking rag gag,
I have bitten through soft lower lip in two places,
my position so tightly maintained.
Mouth like a gutted salmon,
you kneel,
pull my chin up to yours,
lick the salt of my eyelids,
cradle the dead weight head:
you let me know you know that I'm sorry.
I spit out the gag.
You eat me
voraciously –
lower me onto my front
and trail the spatters of purple and red
with swollen fingers.
I wince and shudder,
gooseflesh spreading through spasming limbs:
I am broken
but we both know it's taking me longer and longer each time.

I haven't been sleeping lately.
The nights are heavy,
it hurts to lie on my back:
it's never enough.
I make you bind me and pick out a cane but your heart's not in it;

we quit after six
and settle for cinnamon coffee and *Silver Screen Legends* on
Five.
Old scar gets lost in wrinkle
as you cackle cracked teeth at the telly;
your skin like a bird's nest,
you criss-cross and crease
and even the homemade name on your knuckles
skips back and forth
from Deb to Dee.

You want to put a baby inside me,
you told me this morning.
Oscar
Stanislaus
Popeye.
Unless it's a girl,
in which case you don't know.
You tell me how you will pat and rub my belly,
how you will make me not carry even a tiny potato,
how I will be your Queen and you will be my Slave.
I see.
You will relish this role for a week maybe –
it will lapse
before I am showing.
You will go elsewhere for sex if I lack interest,
give me a list of possible fathers
and interrogate every action.
You'll enforce your right to my anus
– so we don't hurt the baby –
I churn.
I try to picture you at six but there's no mirror to what I imagine;
you have no photos.

We joke on the phone but your voice is thin
and you ask me to send you some money.

You're on remand again,
accused:
a combination of anger and booze,
we assume they'll sentence you this time –
my guts are dancing.
I tell you I'm working.
I smile –
I'm wiping arses in the local old folks' home.
I crook our purple phone to my ear,
trace the line of tiny red dots from my elbow to wrist
– They have industrial cling film dispensers! I say.
I'm straining to crackle your laughter
but nothing will break you.
You tell me you're horny,
so I start to bring myself off, but the credit runs dry;
I come
to an empty line.
I strip
and leave the phone off the hook
whilst I think about painting our bedroom
and nap on and off towards dreams of you,
purple and yellow.

I've decided to test you.
If you don't spot my tactics it means you are using, I reason.
I root out all of the old prison letters you've saved
and copy the first one I find,
word for word,
to a clean sheet of paper.
You said you'd turned a new leaf; well, let's see.
Posted, I buy twenty Marlboros,
finger them,
count them,
crumble them up
and throw them away. My nails stink
but my willpower, fucking amazing.

Court is in twenty-eight days.
I make you a card with paint and glitter,
neon pens
and a snippet of hair from my head.
I consider the option of cutting my limbs off,
one
at a time,
and posting them to you in secret parcels,
one day springing to life like a human jack in your box.
It will not do.
My bruises have faded,
my scratches and weals have healed
and there's no one can kick-start the car like you do.
I use my VO.
Against all the odds I'd stacked, you've noticed my home-made
     drug test
letter repetition.
– You silly girl, you say,
and we laugh till we're crying like earthquakes.
I'm wearing the feathery skirt like you said to.
As planned, you watch
as I lower
fingers
to
crotch
and run through the *Cherry Popper Daddies* C/P DVD I was
     watching last night –
I was thinking of you.
A guard starts to walk our way,
his right arm is raised –
he waves –
head shaking in your direction.
We roll our eyes.
I straighten my feathers and lean to your cheek,
your sweat pure caffeine,
you reek.
– I think I will eat you completely today, I whisper.

I lick
and jump at the whistle.
The hour is over.

Though I'm eating my meals from the bowl on the floor like
    normal,
it's rarely the same.
I used the cardboard copy of you from the last time you left me
    alone at first,
but you slid and tumbled time and again,
a crippled gull fumbling over its prey, you flapped
and slipped
on the lino
and I got sick of propping you up
so I tore off your head in a rage
and set my lighter on it.
With no version of you at all
I can't swallow;
my belly burns with remorse,
I'm knotty,
I vomit every morning into my yoghurt.
What will I tell you?

There is this vulture in me
which the doctor is deaf to.
It scales the cage of my ribs,
it seethes and strangles my too-full womb
and shatters my bowels;
its language is lost.
– Take this pill now and on Thursday return for another,
she says.
– The first will terminate,
the second expel,
so I take the pill I am given and start to wait.

Court is tomorrow.
You're sick of wasting your money

to hear me
heaving tears down the phone
but my throat pulls tight against conversation,
my larynx raw like bloodied bones –
I choke them down.
Rubbed ragged
to gravel,
I'm pocked –
I'm rotting meat every minute –
I'm scratching my ribs until nails are full to the brim with red-
flecked skin –
I'm cracking my shell wide open.
– Salt in the bath to heal a graze, my mother would say.
She packs me away in a suitcase,
she is ashamed in the dream that chases me out of sleep:
A fire.
Four out of five children die and I can't make the new ones in
time.
Their eyes ping out.

The cat seems to have your tongue before the judge and I
can't help but titter.
The notion of you so submissive,
hands like a garland of arthritic buds,
gagged in cuffs
on hips drawn heavy through lack of exertion,
and my glitter betrays the back of your neck,
it bathes in your sweat and makes you
pathetic –
Oh! What a picture!
I laugh so hard my stomach balls up,
my sanitary towel spills over with clots
and snot sprays down from my nose and finds a new home
in between my lips.
I rise,
chest heaving,
keeping my thighs together,

and make my way to the door
where you catch my eye in a second and stop my hysteria dead.

I told you over the phone that night why I couldn't stay at the
    magistrates' court:
it was starting to feel like a squirrel was cramming my skull with
    its nuts
and the fear of my head splitting open was making me twitchy.
You'd called with the verdict,
angry:
– Eighteen months,
you said.
– Piss easy,
you said.
– I'll be out in a year so don't go fucking around,
you said –
and then the money ran out and the line went dead
so that was that
and I tugged out the plug and crushed it under my foot.

As for the bloodied sheets,
and the pills
and the clinic,
I think I'll forget –
I've already forgotten –
I've not once thought of it all day long!
I'll butterfly stitch this slice in my thigh, then bleach out the
toilet;
I'm going to do you proud.
I'll root out my old *Famous Five* books –
I'm going to read them aloud to myself –
each night a new chapter,
like you did
before things got awkward,
but first I must do the important stuff:
I need to polish the paddles and sharpen the knives for when
    you get back.

And that soup I was going to make –
it'll freeze
but all I've got is an onion
and I daren't go out without asking you first
but I need new potatoes
and carrots
and leeks,
and meaty stock to thicken up my water.

RED

Red is danger,
red is light,
red is the traffic lights in the night.
Red is my best colour,
red is the colour of blood,
red might not be your best colour
but red is the colour I love.
Come on folks,
red's quite nice,
at least red is better than mice.
I always water my red rose;
to you, red is horrid I suppose.

By Rosy Leaver

ACKNOWLEDGEMENTS

I am very grateful to James Burt, for helping me edit these poems and for living through them with me over the last twelve years. I am also grateful to Ashley Clark, for designing the book cover and for being such a wonderful friend.

Thank you to everyone else who has inspired, supported, discussed, critiqued, published, listened to and otherwise engaged with the poems in this collection, and to all those who love me and look after me. In particular:

Hannah Ayin, Ros Barber, Olive Carrick, Polly Carrick, Anna Carrick-Leaver, Edward Carrick-Leaver, Carol Divall, Nathan Filer, Toni Griffiths, Jamie Harrison, Alice Helps, Cleria Humphries, Peter Hunter, Sally Jenkinson, Robin Lawley, Debby Leaver, Mark Leaver, Norman Leaver, Sam Leaver, Joe Luna, Hollie McNish, Mike Parker, Chris Parkinson, Rosie Phillips-Leaver, Kitty Peels, Ashley, Benjamin, Eleanor, Faye, Jennifer, Mike, Sylvia, Vicky and Zoe Pittman, Kate Shields, Year Solver, Jake Spicer, Verity Spott, Keston Sutherland, Sam Turton, Erika Walker, Rachel Weston, Juliette Wright, and Sam and Aidan Wright.

I especially want to thank Luke Wright. For your support, your kindness, your company, your perversity, for every cell of your brilliant existence and for that time you started off the clapping on the plane when I thought it wasn't worth doing anymore, I love you.